Python Programming for Beginners

The Complete Beginners Guide

Koso Brown

Table of Contents

Introduction

Find out about the need for Python abilities, its uses, and how to learn the language. With the help of our extensive guide, get started with Python right now.

Python is among the most widely used programming languages, so a lot of people are interested in learning it. However, what is the process for initiating? This book covers all the information you require to start your learning process, including a detailed learning plan and step-by-step instructions, as well as some of the best tools available to support your success.

Chapter 1: What is Python?

Guido van Rossum invented Python, a high-level interpreted programming language, which was initially made available in 1991. Because of its syntax, programmers can express concepts in less lines of code than they might in languages like Java or C++. It is created with code readability in mind.

Multiple programming paradigms, such as procedural, object-oriented, and functional programming, are supported by Python. To put it simply, this means that you can write code in a variety of ways using its flexibility, such as procedural programming, object-oriented programming, or functional programming, which involves treating your code like a math problem.

It is used for:

- ❖ mathematics
- ❖ software development
- ❖ web development (server-side)
- ❖ system scripting

Why is Python such a popular language?

Python continues to be the most widely used programming language as of July 2023, per the TIOBE index. Python's ease of use, adaptability, and variety of uses have made it one of the most widely used programming languages across time.

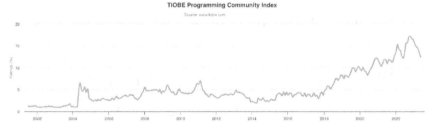

Due to these factors, data scientists also find it to be a highly preferred language since it frees them up to concentrate more on interpreting data than on linguistic nuances.

Python's primary characteristics

Let's examine some of the characteristics of Python that contribute to its popularity and versatility as a programming language:

1. **Open source and free.** Additionally, the language is open-source, meaning that anybody may download, share, and alter its source code without restriction. As a result, a sizable developer community has contributed to its growth and established a broad network of Python libraries.

2. **Dynamically typed.** Because Python is dynamically typed, variables don't require you to specify their data type at creation. Because the type is inferred by the Python interpreter, the code is more versatile and user-friendly.

3. **Platform independence.** The language's ability to allow you to create code once and have it work on any operating system is one of its best features. Python is an excellent option if you collaborate with people that use different operating systems because of its functionality.

4. **Interpreted language.** Python is an interpreted language, meaning that each line of code is carried out individually. Because you can test individual lines of code without needing to build the entire program, this can facilitate debugging.

5. **Rich library support.** You can save time and effort by using the extensive standard library that contains pre-written code for a variety of activities. Further expanding Python's capability are thousands of third-party packages created by the active Python community.

6. **Platform independence.** The language's ability to allow you to create code once and have it work on any operating system is one of its best features. Python is an excellent option if you collaborate with people that use different operating systems because of its functionality.

7. **Easy to learn.** Because of its readability, Python is a very easy language for beginners to learn and comprehend what the code does.

8. **Versatility.** Python is useful in many different fields and is not restricted to just one kind of task. Python has the tools to help you achieve your goals, whether they include web development, task automation, or data science exploration.

9. **Readability.** Python is renowned for having a syntax that is easy to understand and somewhat similar to English.

Why is learning Python so beneficial?

Gaining knowledge of Python has several advantages. Python has applications in a wide range of areas, including tech, finance, healthcare, and more, in addition to its widespread popularity. Gaining proficiency in Python ensures better professional outcomes and opens up a wide range of career options. How to do it is as follows:

1. **Python is used in many different contexts.**

Although Python's adaptability has already been discussed, let's examine a few concrete applications for it:

- **AI and machine learning.** PyTorch, Scikit-learn, TensorFlow, and other libraries make Python a popular choice in this sector.
- **creation of games.** With the help of libraries like PyGame and tkinter, you may even utilize it for game development.

- **software engineering.** Python can be used for testing, automation, and scripting in software development.

- **web creation.** Backend web development uses frameworks like Flask and Django.

- **Data science.** Python is a popular language for data analysis and visualization, and tools like Matplotlib, NumPy, and Pandas are especially helpful.

2. Python expertise is in high demand.

Python expertise is in high demand due to the growth of data science, machine learning, and artificial intelligence. Python is now the third most popular language on GitHub, with usage rising 22.5% year, according to a 2022 report from the company.

Businesses in a wide range of sectors are looking for experts who can use Python to automate processes, create machine learning models, and extract insights from data. Certification in Python is also in demand.

Gaining knowledge of Python can greatly increase your employability and lead to a variety of job prospects. Approximately 10,000 jobs in the US require Python, according to a fast search for the talent on the employment website Indeed.

Chapter 2: How Much Time Is Needed to Learn Python?

Even though Python is one of the simpler programming languages to learn, commitment and repetition are still necessary. Depending on your past programming experience, the difficulty of the topics you're trying to understand, and the amount of time you have available to study, learning Python can take a variety of lengths of time.

On the other hand, you can typically understand the fundamentals in a few weeks and reach a moderate level of proficiency in a few months with a disciplined learning strategy and constant effort.

The breadth and depth of online information can provide you with a solid foundation for your abilities. For instance, it takes about 24 study hours to finish our Python Programming skill track, which covers the skills required to code effectively, and about 36 study hours to complete our Data Analyst with Python career track. Naturally, being a true Pythonista takes time, and a large portion of your efforts will need to be self-study in addition to more structured approaches.

In contrast to other languages, the following is a time comparison of learning Python:

LANGUAGE	TIME TO LEARN
PYTHON	Basics take 1-3 months, while advanced subjects take 4–12 months.
JULIA	Basics take 1-3 months, while advanced subjects take 4–12 months.
R	Basic subjects take 1-3 months, whereas advanced subjects take 4–12 months.
	1-3 months for advanced subjects, and one to two

SQL	months for fundamentals

The timelines for learning to become proficient in a programming language are the only basis for the above comparisons; they do not represent timelines for breaking into a profession. Furthermore, since everyone learns differently and progresses at their own rate, these timetables are merely meant to serve as a framework.

Methods for Learning Python

Let's examine the steps involved in learning Python. You will need to start from the very beginning and work your way up because this instructional guide assumes you are a beginner learning Python.

1. Recognize the purpose behind your Python study

First and first, it's critical to ascertain your reasons for wishing to learn Python. It's a very adaptable language with a wide range of uses. Thus, knowing your motivation for studying Python will enable you to create a customized study schedule.

Whether your interest lies in software development, data analysis, or task automation, having a specific objective in mind can help you stay motivated and focused on your learning process. You could ask yourself the following questions:

- **What career objectives do I have?** Are you interested in pursuing a career in software engineering, web development, data science, or another area where Python is frequently utilized?

- **What is my level of skill right now?** Python's ease of use and readability make it an excellent first language for beginners. Python has strong libraries and frameworks, which may pique the interest of seasoned programmers.

- **What piques my curiosity?** Do you want to create applications or work with data? Or maybe artificial intelligence intrigues you? Your educational path may be influenced by your interests.

- **What issues am I attempting to resolve?** Do you want to construct a website, analyze data, automate processes, or develop a machine learning model? You can use Python for all of these things and much more.

Your learning path's structure will be determined by the answers to these questions, which is crucial for the phases that follow.

One of the simplest programming languages to learn is Python. The great thing about learning Python is that it doesn't force you to stick to just one field—it can be used for data research, artificial intelligence, software development, and nearly any other job that involves programming!

2. Start by learning the basic principles of Python

Python places a strong emphasis on the readability of code and lets you express ideas in fewer lines of code. It is advisable to commence by grasping fundamental ideas like variables, data types, and operators.

- **Setting up your environment and installing Python**

Python installation and development environment setup are prerequisites for beginning Python coding. Utilizing Anaconda Python, you can start using Python in your browser by downloading it from the official website.

- **Compose your first Python program.**

Write a basic Python program to begin with, like the traditional "Hello, World!" script. This procedure will assist you in comprehending the syntax and organization of Python programming.

- **Python data structures**

Numerous built-in data structures, including sets, dictionaries, tuples, and lists, are available in Python. In your programs, these data structures are used to store and handle data.

- **Python's control flow**

Programs that use control flow statements, such as if-statements, for-loops, and while-loops, can make decisions and repeat operations.

- **Python functions**

Python functions are units of reusable code that carry out

particular tasks. Both custom and pre-built Python routines are available.

3. Understand intermediate Python fundamentals

After mastering the fundamentals, you can begin exploring some more complex subjects. Once more, these are crucial for deepening your grasp of Python and will assist you in resolving a variety of issues and scenarios that may arise when utilizing the programming language.

❖ Exceptions and error reporting

Python gives you the capabilities to manage exceptions and errors in your programming. To write robust Python programs, you must know how to raise exceptions and use try/except blocks.

❖ Using Python libraries

Python's extensive library ecosystem is what gives it its power. Discover how to import and utilize popular libraries such as matplotlib for data visualization, pandas for data processing, and numpy for numerical calculation.

❖ Python object-oriented programming

Object-oriented programming (OOP) is a paradigm that lets

14

you organize your code around classes and objects, and Python supports it. Having a solid understanding of OOP ideas like inheritance, polymorphism, classes, and objects will help you write more structured and effective code.

4. Gain knowledge by doing

Using Python actively is one of the best methods to learn it. Reduce the amount of time you spend studying syntax and get started on tasks as soon as you can. Using a learn-by-doing methodology, you apply the concepts you've learned in the classroom to practical projects and exercises.

Here are some additional methods for honing your abilities:

- **Utilize the knowledge you've gained to your own concepts and endeavors.** Attempt to replicate completed tasks or helpful tools that you locate. Since you have to figure out how something works and how to apply it yourself, this may be a great learning experience.
- **Take on challenging projects.** Take up projects that pique your interest. This might be a web application, a

data analysis project, or just a straightforward script to automate a task.

- **Take part in code-along and webinars.** Learning new ideas and seeing how they're used in practice can be greatly facilitated by this approach.

5. Create a portfolio of your work

As you finish your assignments, gather them into a portfolio. Your abilities and interests should be reflected in this portfolio, which should also be customized to the industry or career you're interested in. Make an effort to add uniqueness to your work and demonstrate your ability to solve problems.

Here are some suggested projects for various skill levels:

- **Beginners.** easy projects like a to-do list app, a number guessing game, or a simple data analysis with a dataset you are interested in.
- **Intermediate.** progressively more complicated tasks, such as web scrapers, Django-powered blog websites, or Scikit-learn-powered machine learning models.
- **Advanced.** large-scale initiatives like a deep learning model with PyTorch or TensorFlow, a complicated data analysis project, or a full-stack web application.

6. Continue to push yourself

Never give up learning. Look for projects and tasks that are more difficult after you've mastered the fundamentals. Concentrate on topics that are related to your interests or professional aspirations. In the realm of Python, there's always more to learn, be it machine learning, web development, or data science. Recall that learning Python is a journey rather than a sprint. Practice often, maintain your curiosity, and don't be scared to make errors.

Chapter 3: How to Set Up Python on Windows and macOS

This comprehensive guide will teach you how to install Python on your computer. Learn many ways to begin using Python on your computer, regardless of whether you use Windows or macOS.

Python is a potent, all-purpose programming language that's popular in data research, artificial intelligence, scientific computing, and web development. Python installation is required if you're new to programming and want to get started with it on your PC.

This guide will show you how to install Python on Windows and Mac using several approaches, find out what version of Python is installed on your computer, and get started with Python. Additionally, we will demonstrate how to install Python packages, which are necessary for any Python development project.

1. **Installing Python on a macOS**

Like installing Python on a Windows computer, installing Python can be done in a number of ways, which this guide will cover:

- **Install Python from the Python website directly:** You may personalize your installation and have control over the installation process with this option.
- **Use the Anaconda distribution to install Python:** Anaconda is a well-liked Python distribution that has a ton of pre-installed tools and packages, which makes it a fantastic choice for data research and scientific computing.

2. **Verifying Whether Python Is Already Installed on Your macOS**

Use these steps to see if Python is installed on your macOS computer:

- Navigating to the Applications folder or using Spotlight search to look up Terminal will launch the app.
- Enter python3 into the command line. If Python is installed, the Python prompt, which looks like this

">>>," should appear after a notification stating something like "Python 3.x.x." The version number of Python is "3.x.x".

- An error message claiming that Python cannot be found will appear if Python is not installed on your computer.

How to Install Python from the Python Website on macOS

Use the complete Python installer from the Python website to install Python on your macOS computer by following these steps:

- ❖ Go to the Python download page.
- ❖ Under the "Python Releases for macOS" section, click the link for the latest version of Python (e.g., At the time of writing, the latest version of Python is Python 3.11.1).
- ❖ On the Python download page, in the "Files" section, click on "macOS 64-bit universal2 installer".
- ❖ Once the download is complete, double-click the file to begin the installation process.
- ❖ Complete the installation by clicking on Continue and ticking the license agreement until the installer starts extracting files and the installation process is complete.

You may need to provide your admin password to complete the installation.

❖ To exit the installer after the installation is finished, click the "Close" button.

❖ To verify that Python has been installed correctly, follow the directions in the section "Checking if Python is Already Installed on Your macOS Machine" after the installation is finished.

How to Use Anaconda to Install Python on macOS

Different Python distributions have the necessary tools and packages pre-installed. With a plethora of data science tools and packages pre-installed, the Anaconda Python installation is one of the most widely used distributions. Use an Anaconda distribution to download Python by doing the following steps:

❖ Find out what kind of CPU your Mac has. Choose "About This Mac" by clicking on the Apple logo located in the upper left corner of your desktop. Note the value in the "Chip" row in the Overview pane.

❖ Visit the download page for Anaconda.

❖ Scroll down to the "Anaconda Installers" section — there, you will find different versions of the Anaconda

Installer. If your Mac has a CPU of type "Apple M1", click on "64-Bit (M1) Graphical Installer". Otherwise click on "64-Bit Graphical Installer".

❖ Double-clicking the downloaded file will launch the installation procedure.

❖ After the installer begins extracting files and the installation process is finished, click Continue and check the license agreement to finish the installation.

❖ You will also be prompted to install JetBrains' DataSpell data science IDE after the installation is finished.

❖ You will get a screen that reads "Installation was completed successfully" if the installation is successful. Click "Finish."

❖ To verify that Python has been installed correctly, follow the directions in the section "Checking if Python is Already Installed on Your macOS Machine" after the installation is finished.

Installing Python on a Windows Computer

Python can be installed on a Windows computer in a few different methods. The choices we'll look at in this session are listed below:

1. **Install Python from the Microsoft Store directly:** You can quickly become proficient with Python with this simple and quick solution. For novices who wish to utilize Python on their computer for learning, it is really helpful.

2. **Install Python straight from the Python website:** This approach lets you personalize your installation and offers you further control over the procedure.

3. **Use the Anaconda distribution to install Python:** Anaconda is a well-liked Python distribution that has a ton of pre-installed tools and packages, which makes it a fantastic choice for data research and scientific computing.

Regardless of the approach you select, you can begin utilizing Python on your Windows computer in a couple of steps. On sometimes, Python may come pre-installed on your computer. Here's how to find out if Python is installed on your Windows computer.

Checking to See Whether Python Is Installed on Your Windows Computer

You can use the Start Menu or the terminal to access Python.

Use the terminal to verify whether Python is installed on your

Windows computer by doing the following steps:

- Launch a command line utility, like Command Prompt (the default on Windows 10) or Windows Terminal (the default on Windows 11).

- Enter {python} into the command line. If Python is installed, the Python prompt, which looks like this ">>>," should appear after a notification stating something like "Python 3.x.x." Keep in mind that "3.x.x" is the Python version number.

- You will be sent to the Python installation page on the Microsoft Store if Python is not already installed on your computer. Be aware that Python may not be at its most recent version on the page you are taken to.

- Use the Start Menu to see if Python is installed on your Windows computer. To do so, perform the following:

- To access the Start Menu, either click the Start button or press the Windows key.

- Put "python" in the search bar.

- Python should appear as the best match if it is installed. To launch the desired version of Python, click or press "Enter". The Python prompt, which appears like this ">>>," should appear after a message stating something like "Python 3.x.x." Keep in mind that "3.x.x" is the Python version number.
- You will only see results from web searches for "python" or a recommendation to look for "python" in the Microsoft Store if Python is not installed on your computer.

Chapter 4: How to Use the Microsoft Store to Install Python on Windows

Use the Microsoft Store to install Python on your Windows computer by following these steps:

1. On your Windows computer, launch the Microsoft Store application. To accomplish this, search for "Microsoft Store" in the Start menu.

2. Use the Microsoft Store app to look up "Python." Several "Python X.X" apps ought to appear in the search results. The variations of Python that are accessible on the Microsoft shop are denoted by X.X. Generally speaking, opt for the most recent version of Python, which is 3.11 as of this writing.

3. To access the app page, click on the app.

4. To start the installation procedure, click the "Get" button.

5. Python will be downloaded and installed on your computer by the Microsoft Store. Depending on the speed of your internet connection, this could take a few minutes.

6. To verify that Python has been installed correctly, follow the directions in the section "Checking if Python is

Already Installed on Your Windows Machine" after the installation is finished.

7. he IDLE Shell, a straightforward IDE for executing Python commands, is also included with this Python installation. Look for the IDLE Shell in the Start menu's all apps section to get access to it.

https://apps.microsoft.com/detail/9PJPW5LDXLZ5?hl=en-us&gl=US

Click this link to install Python from the Microsoft Store.

How to Download and Install Python from the Python Website on Windows

Use the complete Python installer from the Python website to install Python on your Windows computer by following these steps:

- ❖ Visit the link to get Python.
- ❖ Click the link for the most recent version of Python under the "Python Releases for Windows" section (for example, Python 3.11.1 is the most recent version as of this writing).
- ❖ Select the "Windows installer (64-bit)" version of Python from the download page.
- ❖ Start the installer file to start the installation procedure after the download is finished.
- ❖ You will see an option to "Add Python 3.x to PATH" once the installer opens. This is only advised if you wish to use Python from the terminal (instead of an IDE) and you are installing a single version of the language rather than several versions.
- ❖ To start the installation, click the "Install Now" button. A few minutes will pass during the installation procedure. Be aware that you might be prompted to select the features you wish to have installed before selecting "Install Now." It is advised that you go with the default installation unless you have particular modification requests.

- ❖ 'Disable path length limit' will be an option presented to you after the installation is finished. While this is not necessary for everyday Python use, it is advised for Python development since it can help avoid issues with lengthy auto-generated file paths.
- ❖ To end the installation, click the "Close" button.
- ❖ To verify that Python has been installed correctly, follow the directions in the section "Checking if Python is Already Installed on Your Windows Machine" after the installation is finished.

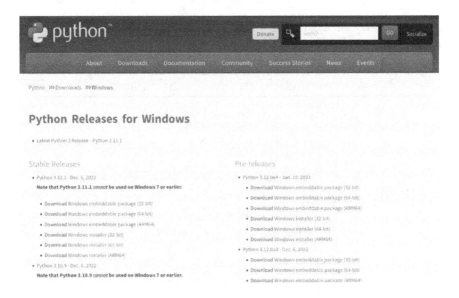

https://www.python.org/downloads/windows/

Go here to access the Python Site Installation.

How to Use Anaconda to Install Python on Windows

Different Python distributions have the necessary tools and packages pre-installed. With a plethora of data science tools and packages pre-installed, the Anaconda Python installation is one of the most widely used distributions. Use an Anaconda distribution to download Python by doing the following steps:

1. Go to https://www.anaconda.com/download
2. You can find various versions of the Anaconda Installer by scrolling down to the "Anaconda Installers" section. To install the most recent version of Python on Windows, click on the "64-Bit Graphical Installer" for Python 3.9 at the time of writing.
3. Save the installer file to your computer. Click the installer to begin the installation after the download is complete.
4. Double-clicking the downloaded file will launch the installation procedure.
5. After the installer begins extracting files and the installation process is finished, click Continue and check the license agreement to finish the installation.

6. You can "Add Anaconda3 to my PATH environment variable" from the "Advanced Installations Options" box. This is only advised if you wish to use the conda tool from the terminal (instead of an IDE) and you only have one installation of Anaconda Python (instead of several versions).

7. The installation procedure will begin when the installer extracts the files. This could require many minutes. You will be prompted to install JetBrains' DataSpell data science IDE optionally when the installation is finished.

8. A "Thanks for installing Anaconda" screen will appear after the installation is accomplished. Click "Finish."

9. To verify that Python has been installed correctly, follow the directions in the section "Checking if Python is Already Installed on Your Windows Machine" after the installation is finished.

https://www.anaconda.com/download

Go here to access the Python Anaconda installation.

Best Practices for Learning Python

These suggestions will help you stay focused and make the most of your efforts if you're excited to begin studying Python.

1. Practice frequently

When learning a new language, consistency is essential, and Python is no different. Even if it's only for a little while each day, try to code. Your ability to remember and apply what you've learned will be strengthened by this consistent exercise.

Working on challenging projects or picking up new ideas every day aren't prerequisites for daily practice. It may be as easy as going over what you've learned again, rewriting some of your earlier code, or figuring out difficult coding problems.

2. Select Your Area of Interest

Python is an adaptable language with many uses, including data analysis, machine learning, artificial intelligence, and web development. It can be helpful to concentrate on one subject as you begin your Python journey. This might be determined by your ideal job path, your hobbies, or just what excites you the most.

Your learning can be guided and made more manageable by selecting a focus. For instance, you might give learning libraries like pandas and NumPy top priority if data science is your area of interest. If you want to develop websites, you should concentrate on frameworks like Flask or Django. Recall that picking a focus does not impose restrictions on you. Because of Python's adaptability, knowledge gained in one field may frequently be applied to other ones. As you become more proficient with Python, you can begin branching out and developing new abilities.

3. Join a community

Like any other new ability, learning Python doesn't have to be done alone. In actuality, there are numerous advantages to becoming a part of a community of learners. It can provide chances to learn from others, encourage you to keep going, and offer support when you're encountering difficulties.

You can participate in a variety of Python communities. Local Python meetups provide an in-person opportunity to interact with other Python aficionados, while online forums offer a platform for exchanging knowledge, asking questions, and learning from the experiences of others.

4. Work on real projects

Utilizing Python is the greatest method to learn it. Applying the ideas, you've learnt and gaining practical experience are made possible by working on actual projects. As your skills develop, progressively move on to more complicated tasks from simple ones that serve to reinforce the fundamentals. This might be anything from developing a little game to automating a straightforward chore or even starting a data analysis project.

5. Continue to iterate

Iteration is a key component in learning Python. Review completed tasks or exercises as you get more experience and attempt to make them better or do them in a new way. This could entail adding a new feature, streamlining your code, or simply just making it easier to read. This iterative method will demonstrate your progress over time and serve to reinforce the lessons you've learnt.

6. Never hurry

Python is just another language that requires time to learn. Don't try to learn everything at once by speeding through the content. Prior to going on to the next topic, give each one careful thought. Recall that understanding an idea thoroughly is more important than speeding through the content.

Chapter 5: The Best Careers in Python

Python programming language proficiency is becoming more and more in-demand, as seen by the variety of positions that call for it. Here are a few of the best Python-using occupations you can choose from:

1. A machine learning engineer

Sophisticated programmers that create devices and systems with learning and application capabilities are known as machine learning engineers. Developing algorithms and programs that let robots act without having to be explicitly told to is the responsibility of these experts.

❖ **Key skills:**
- competency with R, SQL, and Python
- profound comprehension of machine learning algorithms
- Understanding of deep learning frameworks (such as TensorFlow)

❖ **Essential tools:**
- Tools for data visualization (such as Matplotlib and Seaborn)
- Machine learning libraries (such as PyTorch, TensorFlow, and Scikit-learn)

- Frameworks for deep learning, such as TensorFlow, Keras, and PyTorch
- Tools for manipulating and analyzing data (e.g., pandas, NumPy)

2. Data analyst

The task of evaluating data and transforming it into knowledge that can suggest improvements for a company falls to data analysts. They compile data from a range of sources and analyze trends and patterns. Following the collection and interpretation of data, data analysts can inform the larger organization of their findings to impact strategic choices.

❖ **Key skills:**
- Good presentation and communication abilities
- proficiency in SQL, R, and Python
- knowledge of data collecting and cleaning methods
- familiarity with business analytics software, such as Tableau and Power BI
- strong proficiency with statistical analysis

❖ **Essential tools:**
- Tools for data analysis (e.g., NumPy, pandas)
- Spreadsheet programs (like Microsoft Excel)
- SQL databases, such as PostgreSQL and MySQL

- Data tools for business intelligence (such as Tableau and Power BI)

3. Data scientist

The detectives of the data world, data scientists are in charge of organizing massive data sets, finding and analyzing rich data sources, and combining disparate data points to spot patterns.

They gather, examine, and understand huge datasets by applying their programming, statistical, and analytical abilities. They then apply this knowledge to provide data-driven answers to difficult business issues.

Creating machine learning algorithms that produce new insights (like identifying consumer segments), automate corporate operations (like predicting credit scores), or offer customers newer value (like recommender systems) is a component of these solutions.

- ❖ **Key skills:**
- Good presentation and communication abilities
- Techniques for reporting and data visualization
- strong familiarity in SQL, R, and Python
- competence in predictive modeling, quantitative analytics, and statistical analysis
- Knowledge of AI and machine learning principles

❖ **Essential tools:**

- Tools for the command line (e.g., Git, Bash)

- Frameworks for big data (like Airflow and Spark)

- Tools for data visualization (such as Tableau and Matplotlib)

- Tools for data analysis (e.g., NumPy, pandas)

- Machine learning libraries (Scikit-learn, for example)

4. Python programmer

Writing server-side web application logic is under the purview of Python developers. They create the application's back-end elements, link it to other online services, and assist front-end developers by fusing their work with the Python program. Python programmers frequently use the robust Python library ecosystem to their advantage while working in data analysis and machine learning.

❖ **Key skills:**

- a fundamental knowledge of database technology, such as PostgreSQL and MySQL

- Knowledge of ORM libraries

- familiarity with Python web frameworks, such as Flask and Django

- Knowledge of front-end technologies (JavaScript, HTML, CSS)
- proficiency with the Python programming language

❖ **Essential tools:**

- Python web development libraries (such as Flask and Django)
- Version control systems (Git, for example)
- Python IDEs, such as PyCharm

Conclusion

Acquiring knowledge of Python can lead to numerous professional prospects and is a fulfilling experience. This guide has given you a road map for beginning your Python learning journey, from grasping the fundamentals to becoming proficient in more complex ideas and working on practical projects.

To learn Python or any other programming language, keep in mind that practice and consistency are essential. Take your time going over the principles. Spend some time learning each one and putting it to use in real-world tasks. Take part in coding challenges, interact with Python communities, and never stop learning.